For My Children

Selected Teachings

Of

MATA AMRITANANDAMAYI

Translation by

Brahmachari Ramakrishna Chaitanya

MATA AMRITANANDAMAYI CENTER
San Ramon, California

FOR MY CHILDREN
Selected Teachings Of
Mata Amritanandamayi

PUBLISHED BY:
Mata Amritanandamayi Center
P.O. Box 613
San Ramon, CA 94583-0613
Tel: 510-537-9417

ALSO AVAILABLE FROM:
Mata Amritanandamayi Mission Trust
Amritapuri P.O.
Kollam Dt., Kerala 690525 INDIA

ISBN 1-879410-61-3

Contents

Introduction

The gift of India to the world is her culture of Self-Realization, her vision of raising man to the heights of God-consciousness. The West, disillusioned with the empty grandeur of materialism, looks to the perennial philosophies of the East for guidance and refuge. From ancient times to the present day, an unbroken succession of God-Realized souls have taken birth in India to lead seekers of Truth to their goal.

It is not surprising that some self-seeking individuals have put on the garb of enlightened masters to take advantage of the Western thirst for spiritual guidance. The West has suffered much from this deception and has developed a paranoia toward 'Gurus'. Because of a few charlatans, we need not lose faith that genuine Masters exist. Because some quacks are practicing medicine, do we cease to look for a reputable doctor to free us from our illness?

"Why does one need a spiritual guide?" you may ask. "After reading a few books, can't I make my own way along the spiritual path?"

If one desires to become a doctor, one must study under the instruction of learned professors. Even after graduating from medical school, one interns in a hospital under the guidance of practicing doctors. We spend many years to fulfill our dream of becoming a doctor. What then of aspiring to realize the Supreme Truth? If we desire spiritual wisdom, we must seek out true spiritual Masters who have studied, practiced and experienced Truth.

What distinguishes a true teacher from an imposter? In the Presence of an Enlightened Being, one feels a tangible aura of love and tranquillity. We can observe the equal treatment that all receive regardless of status or fortune, religion or race, from one immersed in Divinity. Each word and action of a true Master serves to awaken people spiritually. No trace of ego or selfishness exists in a Mahatma, who, with open arms, receives and serves all.

An ideal example of such a teacher is Mata Amritanandamayi, the Mother of Immortal Bliss. Born in 1953, Ammachi, as she is called, is revered as the embodiment of the Universal Mother. This book contains selections from her spiritual teachings and answers to frequent questions of seekers. Mother's words are the simple words of a village girl yet reveal the profound understanding of one speaking from Divine Experience. Her counsels are universal and applicable to our daily lives whether we are serious spiritual aspirants, householders or sceptics.

Most of all, Mother's teachings demand that we think. These are not flowery utterances that spoon-feed our mind and intellect. On the contrary, one must contemplate her words in order to plumb their full meaning. At times, a saying may seem incomplete or not thoroughly explained. When Mother is sometimes consulted for further elaboration, she says, "Let them think it over." That is to say, the principles that she expounds need contemplation, not excessive explanation. If one is serious about Self-Realization and dedicates oneself with sincerity and humility to the study and practice of these teachings, one can definitely reach the goal. Open this book to a random page and see how Mother's words speak to you.

A Sketch Of Amma's Life

"From birth I had an intense love of the Holy Name of God. I would repeat the Lord's Name incessantly with every breath. Divine thoughts constantly flowed in my mind no matter the place where I was or the work I was doing."

Born on September 27, 1953, in a remote village along the southwest coast of India, Sudhamani (Ambrosial Jewel), as she was named by her humble parents, bore signs of divinity from her birth. She was born with an unusual dark blue complexion, the color of Krishna and Kali. The doctors forbade her parents to wash her for several months, hoping to cure the mysterious 'disease'. Sudhamani started to pick-up her mother tongue, Malayalam, when she was barely six months old, and started walking at that age, without having first crawled on all fours.

From the age of five she began composing many songs in praise of Sri Krishna, full of divine love and poignant with longing for her Beloved. The verses, though childlike in their innocent simplicity, were not without mystical and philosophical depth. She became well known in the village for these songs and for her beautiful voice. In her ninth year she had to leave school, because her mother fell ill and could no longer do the house work. Getting up before dawn and working until eleven at night, she cooked for the entire family, tended the ten cows, washed all the clothes, kept the house and yard tidy, and ministered to the old and ill of the village. In spite of the long workdays, whatever time she could spare she spent in heartfelt song and prayers to Lord Krishna.

Before long she had many divine visions, and by the time she was seventeen her state of bliss deepened into permanent union with the Divine. She viewed the world as the manifestation of the all-pervading One. The mere mention of God's Name would plunge her mind into deep absorption.

At this time a strong desire arose in her to realize the Divine Mother. Seeking Her Vision, she undertook severe austerities, refusing food and shelter for some months. Finally the Divine Mother appeared to her, then became an effulgence and merged in her. Sudhamani's face shown with divine splendour. She felt no inclination to be with people, spending her time in solitude enjoying the Bliss of God-Realization.

However, one day she heard a voice within her say, "You have not been born simply to enjoy bliss and peace for yourself, but rather to give comfort and solace to suffering humanity. Use your divine gifts to relieve people. That will be the real worship of Me, who resides in the hearts of all beings as their Essence." From that day on Sudhamani, now reverently addressed as 'Amma' or 'Ammachi' (Mother), devoted herself to the welfare of mankind. Whoever comes to her, spiritual or worldly, she receives tenderly, patiently listens to their problems, comforts them as only a mother can do, and uses her divine power to relieve them.

Mother says, "Different types of people come to see me, some out of devotion, others for a solution to their worldly problems, for relief from diseases, etc. I discard none. Can I reject them? Are they different from me ? Are not we all beads strung on the same Life Thread ? According to their level of thinking they see me. Both those who love me and those who hate me are the same to me."

On Mother

Children, the mother who gave birth to you may look after matters relating to this life. These days even this is very rare. But Mother's aim is to lead you in such a way that you can enjoy bliss in all your future lives.

When the pus in a wound is squeezed out, it causes pain; but will a sincere doctor refrain from doing this just because it is painful? In the same way, when your *vasanas*,(innate tendencies from the past), are being removed, you feel pain. This pain is for your good. Just as the pests that destroy the sprouting plant are removed, Mother is removing the bad *vasanas* in you.

It may be easy for you to love Mother, but that is not enough. Try to see Mother in everyone. Oh, my Children, don't think that Mother is confined to this body alone.

To love Mother truly means to love equally all beings in the world.

The love of those who love Mother only when Mother loves them is not real. Only when one can cling to Mother's feet in spite of her scoldings does one truly love Mother.

One who lives in this Ashram and leads one's life following Mother's every instruction can become liberated. If Mother's deeds and words are contemplated, not a single scripture need be studied.

The mind must hold onto something. This is not possible without faith. When a seed is sown, its upward growth depends upon the roots growing deeply into the soil. Without faith, spiritual growth is not possible.

Wherever you go, you must either chant your mantra silently or meditate. If this is not possible, you must read spiritual books. Don't waste time. Mother does not worry about the loss of ten million rupees, but Mother is really concerned about wasting even a single moment. Money can be regained; not time that is lost. Children, always be aware of the value of time.

Children, Mother does not say that you should believe in Mother or in a God in heaven. It is enough to believe in yourself. Everything is there in you.

If you really love Mother, do *sadhana* (spiritual practice) and know your Self. Mother loves you without expecting anything from you. It is enough if I could see my children always enjoying peace oblivious of day or night.

Only when you have selfless love towards even an ant can Mother consider that you truly love her. Mother does not consider other kinds of love as love. Love born out of selfishness is unbearable for Mother.

Mother's nature varies according to your thoughts and actions. The fierce form of the Lord as 'Narasimha' (half man, half lion), as He pounced roaring on the demon king Hiranyakasipu, became peaceful in the presence of His devotee Prahlada. It is according to the different actions of Hiranyakasipu and

Prahlada that God, who is pure and beyond all attributes, adopted two different attitudes. In the same way, Mother's behaviour also changes in relation to the attitude of her children. Mother, whom you see as the embodiment of Love, may at times appear as the Cruel One! This is to correct the errors in the behaviour of her children; the intention is only to make them good.

Guru

Once we know the particular shop from which we can purchase all our requirements, why should we wander among all the shops in the market? It is a waste of time and is of no use. In the same way, if we have found a Guru, we should stop wandering and do *sadhana*, striving to reach the goal.

The Guru himself will come to the seeker. There is no need to wander in search of him, but the seeker should have intense dispassion towards the world.

A Guru is indispensable for a *sadhak* (aspirant). If a child goes near the edge of a pond, the mother points out the danger and leads the child away. In like manner, the Guru gives appropriate instructions when necessary. His attention is always on the disciple.

Even though God is all-pervading, a Guru's presence is unique. Even though the wind blows everywhere, we enjoy coolness only under the shade of a tree. Doesn't the breeze that blows through the leaves of a tree have a soothing effect on those who travel in the hot sun? Similarly, a Guru is necessary for us who live in the scorching heat of worldly existence. The Guru's presence will give us peace and tranquillity.

Children, the stench of excreta will not diminish however long it be exposed to the sun, unless the wind blows over it. Similarly, doing meditation for ages and ages will not remove the *vasanas* unless one lives with the Guru. Guru's grace is necessary. The Guru pours his grace only into the innocent mind.

We must have an attitude of total surrender to the Guru for our spiritual advancement. When a child learns the alphabet, the teacher holds his finger and makes him scrawl on the sand. The movement of the child's finger is controlled by the teacher. But if the child proudly thinks, 'I know everything,' and does not obey the teacher, how can he learn ?

Experiences, indeed, are the Guru for each person. Sorrow, my Children, is the Guru that brings you closer to God.

One should have reverential devotion (bhaya bhakti) toward the Guru. Moreover, one should have a close relationship with the Guru and should feel that the Guru is one's own. The relationship should be like that of a child to its mother. However much a mother may push away the child, it still clings to her. Though reverential devotion will help us to progress spiritually. real benefit can be gained only through a close relationship with the Guru.

Children, simply loving the Guru will not destroy your *vasanas*. Our devotion and faith should be based on the essential principles of spirituality. Dedication of body, mind and intellect is necessary. The *vasanas* can be eradicated by cultivation of faith in the Guru and obedience to the Guru's will.

A seed must be sown in the shade of a tree in order to sprout. When it becomes a seedling, it should be transplanted. Otherwise, it will not grow properly. In the same way, an aspirant must stay with his Guru for some time, at least a minimum of two or three years. After this, he should do his *sadhana* in a lonely place. This is necessary for his spiritual growth.

A real Guru desires only the spiritual growth of the disciple. Tests and trials are given for the disciple's improvement and to remove his weaknesses. A Guru may even blame a disciple for errors he has not committed. Only those who steadily withstand such trials can grow.

The real Guru can be recognised only through experience.

An artificially incubated chicken cannot survive unless the ideal food and environment are provided, whereas a country-bred chicken can live on any food under any circumstances. Children, the *sadhak* who lives with a Guru is like the country chicken. He will have the courage to overcome any situation. Nothing can enslave him. A *sadhak* who has lived with his Guru will always have the strength acquired from the close association with his Guru.

A disciple may have a possessive attitude towards his Guru. This will not get destroyed easily. The disciple may desire to have continual demonstration of his Guru's love. Some disciples may abuse and leave the Guru when they feel they are not getting it. If one wants the love of the Guru, one must serve selflessly.

God's wrath can be appeased, but even God will not pardon the sin arising from the contempt of the Guru.

Guru and God are there within everyone. But in the beginning, an external Guru is necessary. After a certain stage is reached, one can grasp the essential principles from every object and thereby progress. Until a boy becomes aware of his goal, he studies his lessons out of fear of his parents and teachers. Once he becomes conscious of his goal, he studies on his own accord, foregoing sleep and enjoyments like going to the cinema. The fear and reverence toward his parents which he had until then was not a weakness. Children, when the awareness of the Goal dawns, the Guru aspect within also awakens.

Even though one may come in contact

with a Guru, he will be accepted as a disciple only if he is fit. Without Guru's grace, one cannot know the Guru. One who is really in search of the Truth will have humility and simplicity. The Guru's grace will be showered only on such a person. A person full of ego cannot have access to the Guru.

Children, one can say that 'I' and God are one and the same, but a disciple can never say that 'I' and Guru are one. Guru is the one who has awakened the 'I' in 'me'. That greatness will always remain. The disciple should behave accordingly.

Just as the hen protects her newly hatched chicks under her wing, the real Guru will take total care of those who live according to his instructions. He will point out even silly mistakes and correct them immediately. He will not allow an iota of ego to develop. In order to prune one's pride, the Guru may at times act in an apparently cruel manner.

People who see a blacksmith forging a piece of hot iron with his hammer may think he is a cruel person. The iron may also think him a brute. But while dealing each blow, the blacksmith thinks only of the new form which he is bringing out. Children, the real Guru is like the blacksmith.

God

Many people ask, "Is there a God? If so, where ?" Ask them whether the chicken came first or the egg, or whether the coconut or the coconut tree came into existence first. Who can answer such questions? Beyond the coconut and the coconut tree there exists a power which acts as the substratum of both, a power which is beyond words. That is God. Children, the One that is the Primordial Cause of everything is called God.

Children, to deny God is like using the tongue to say, "I have no tongue." Just as a tree is contained in a seed and butter pervades milk, God dwells in everything.

Even though a tree is latent in a seed, in order to germinate the seed must have the humility to be buried under the soil. If the egg is to be hatched, the hen has to incubate it. Patience is necessary. Butter can be separated from milk only when it is set, curdled and churned. Even though God is all pervading, strenuous effort is necessary to realize Him.

God does not manifest where ego and selfishness prevail. If God comes closer to us by a foot because of our sincere prayers, He moves away from us by a thousand feet because of our selfishness. One can jump into a well in no time, but to climb out of it is difficult. Similarly, God's grace, which is hard to obtain, can be lost in a moment.

Children, even if one does penance for

many lives, God-realization is not possible if one has no yearning and pure love for Him.

A woman is looked upon as a sister by her brother, as a wife by her husband, and as a daughter by her father. No matter who looks at her with what viewpoint, she remains one and the same. In the same way, God is only one. Each person sees God in a different way according to his attitude.

God can take any form. When one makes different shapes out of clay like an elephant or a horse, the nature of the clay does not change. All forms are latent in clay which has no form. Similarly, any form can be carved out of wood. We may call the sculptures by name or all of them may be perceived as wood only in essence. In the same way, God is all-pervading and has no attributes. But He reveals Himself according to our conception of Him.

Children, God, by His Will, can assume any form and return to His essential nature just as water becomes ice and again melts back into water.

Water flowing in different directions can be stored in a reservoir when a dam is constructed. Electricity can be generated from the force of the waterfall thus produced. Similarly, if the mind, now wandering among different sense objects, can be trained to concentrate, the Vision of God can be attained through that power of concentration.

Children, once we take refuge in God, we have nothing to fear. God will look after everything. Children play a game called tag. One child chases the others trying to tag one. The others run to evade the child's touch. If any of them touch a certain tree, the one chasing cannot tag him. In the same way, if we hold onto God, nobody can do anything to us.

When a person looks at his father's portrait, he does not think about the artist or the paint, he remembers his father only. In the same manner, a devotee sees God, the Universal Father, in images. An atheist might say that the sculptor should be adored, not the image. He says this only because he does not have a proper conception of God and the principle behind the image.

There is no point in blaming God for evil and the problems in the world. God has shown us the right path to follow and is not responsible for the miseries we create by not following it. A mother tells her child not to walk by the edge of the pond or touch the fire. If the child falls into the pond or burns his hand by ignoring his mother's warning, why blame the mother?

Those who say, "God will do everything," and sit idle are sluggards. The intelligence given by God is for doing every action with discrimination. If we say that God will look after everything, of what use is our intelligence?

Some may argue that if everything is the Will of God, is it not God who makes us commit mistakes? To say so is meaningless. The responsibility of all action done with a sense of ego rests with the doer only and not God. If we really believe that it is God who has made us commit a crime, we should accept the sentence of hanging passed on us by the judge as also coming from God. Is this possible for us?

Children, God-Realization and Self-Realization are the same. The ability to love all, broadmindedness and equanimity, this is God-Realization.

Even if all the beings in the whole world loved us, we would not experience an iota of the bliss we feel from a moment's taste of the Love of God. So great is the bliss we feel from His love that there is nothing to compare with it.

Just because we do not see God, can we argue that there is no God? Many people have never seen their grandfather. Because of that, do they call their father 'One who had no father?'

As children, we ask many questions and

learn everything from our mother. As we grow a little older, we tell our problems to our friends. When we grow up, we confide our sufferings to our spouse. This is the samskara (tendency) which we have developed. We should change this habit. We should confide our sorrows to God. Only when we share our sorrows with somebody, do we feel relieved. Also, it is not possible to grow without a companion. Let that companion and confidant be God.

Today's friend may be tomorrow's enemy. God is the only friend in whom we can take refuge and whom we can trust completely.

Does God gain anything by our believing in Him? Does the sun require candlelight to see his path? Only the believer benefits from his belief. When we watch with faith the worship of God in a temple and witness camphor being burned as an offering to God, it is our mind that attains concentration and peace.

Followers of different religions follow different customs and have different centers of worship. But God is one and the same. Even if milk is called 'pal' in Malayalam and 'dhood' in Hindi, its quality and colour does not change. Christians hail God by the name Christ, and Muslims call Him Allah. The form of Sri Krishna is not the same in Kerala as it is in North India, where He is pictured wearing a turban. Each person understands and worships God according to his culture and inclination. According to the need of the time and various cultures, Great Souls have portrayed the same God in different forms.

In order to raise oneself from identification with the body to the level of the Supreme Self, one should feel the desperation of a person who is trapped in a burning house or one who is drowning in deep waters. Such a person will not have to wait long for the Vision of God.

Children, when we lose a key, we go to a locksmith to have a lock opened. In order to open the lock of attraction and repulsion, one must seek the key which is in the hands of God.

God is the substratum of everything. Love flourishes from faith in God. From love flows the sense of righteousness (dharma), justice and peace. We should be as eager to sympathize with others' sorrows as we are to apply medicine to our own burnt hand. This can be achieved through full faith in God.

Mahatmas &
Incarnations

The same *Atman* which abides in all beings, abides in me as well. Nothing is
different from me. Others' sorrows and
difficulties are mine. One who realizes
this through his own experience is a Jñani
(Man of Wisdom).

The difference between an Incarnation
and a *jiva*, an individual soul, can be compared to the difference between a man
who has an inborn talent for singing and
one who has learned singing. The former
can learn a song just by hearing it once,
whereas the latter takes a long time to
learn it.

Since everything is part of God, everybody is an incarnation. *Jivas*, not knowing that they are part of God, think, "I am the body. This is my house, my property, my wife."

Incarnations have a sense of fullness which others haven't. Since Incarnations are identified with Nature, their mind is not what we usually call 'mind'. All minds are theirs. An Incarnation is Himself a 'Universal Mind'. Incarnations are beyond the pairs of opposites (purity and impurity, joy and sorrow, etc.). The descent of God Himself in human form is called an Incarnation.

No limitations can bind an Incarnation. Incarnations are like the tips of icebergs in the Ocean of *Brahman* (the Absolute). The whole of God's Power cannot be confined to a human body of five or six feet, but God can work at will through this small body. This is the uniqueness of Incarnations.

Incarnations are a great help in bringing people closer to God. It is only for our sake that God assumes a form. Incarnations are not the body even though They appear to be so to us.

Wherever Mahatmas (Great Souls) appear, people gather around them. People are attracted to them like dust to a whirlwind. Their breath and even the very breeze that touches their body is beneficial to the world.

Children, Jesus was crucified and Sri Krishna was killed by an arrow only by their Will. Nobody could approach them except by their Will. They could have burned to ashes those who opposed them, but they didn't. They had assumed a body to set an example for the world. They had come to show what sacrifice means.

A *sannyasi* (monk) is one who has renounced everything. He will endure and forgive the wrongdoings of others and lead them with love along the right path. He exemplifies self-sacrifice. He is always blissful, not depending on external objects for joy. He revels in his own Self.

One who walks holding the hand of a small child, walks slowly with small steps, lest the child trip and fall. In order to inspire people, one leads them from their level. A seeker should never be proud thinking, "I am a *sannyasi*." He should set an ideal for the world.

In His life, Sri Krishna played many roles: cowherd boy, king, messenger, householder and charioteer. He did not remain in an ivory tower saying,"I am the King." Krishna taught each person according to the samskara,(mental disposition), of that person. He led people by moving with each one. Only such souls can lead the world.

There are some who don the ochre robe proudly declaring, "I am a *sannyasi*." They are like wild tuber plants. Both the wild and farm varieties have a similar appearance, but the wild one has no tubers. Ochre is the colour of fire. Only those who have burnt their body consciousness are fit to wear it.

Scriptures

Children, scriptures are the experiences of the sages. They cannot be grasped through intellect. They can be realized only through personal experience.

We need not learn all the scriptures, which are as vast as the ocean. Like pearls of the sea, we need pick up only the essential principles from the scriptures. After sucking the juice out of the sugarcane, we spit out the stalk.

Only the one who has done *sadhana* (spiritual practices) can grasp the subtle nuances of the scriptures.

Mere scriptural study will not lead one to Perfection. To cure a disease, mere reading of the prescription on the medicine bottle will not suffice; the medicine must be consumed. Liberation cannot be attained by mere study of scriptures; practice is essential.

Practicing meditation along with scriptural study is better than meditating without the aid of scriptural knowledge. When the mind gets agitated, one who has a scriptural background can regain strength through reflection on the words of the scriptures. They help him to overcome his weaknesses. Only one who does *sadhana* coupled with scriptural study can really serve the world selflessly.

Scriptural study is necessary to a certain extent. One who has studied agriculture can easily cultivate a coconut tree. But by merely drawing a picture of a coconut, we cannot quench our thirst. To have coconuts, one must plant and nurture the seedling of a coconut tree. In order to have the experience of all that is described in the scriptures, one must do *sadhana*.

The one who spends his time gaining bookish knowledge of the scriptures without doing *sadhana* is like a fool who tries to live in the blueprint of a house.

If the route is known, the journey will be easy and one will reach the destination quickly. Children, this is the usefulness of the scriptures.

One who has chosen spiritual life should
not spend more than three hours a day
in scriptural studies. The rest of his time
should be spent in *japa*,(repetition of
Lord's name), and meditation.

Excessive indulgence in scriptural study
prevents one from being able to sit in
meditation. One will always have a desire
to teach people. One will think, "I am
Brahman. Why should I meditate?" Even
if one tries to sit for meditation, the mind
will not allow it and will compel one
to get up.

Children, what are you going to gain
by spending your whole life studying the
scriptures? No one would eat a whole
sack of sugar to know it's taste; a pinch
would be enough.

A grain in the granary has the attitude
that it is self-sufficient. It thinks, "Why
should I bow down to the soil?" It does
not think that by coming out of the
granary and germinating, it could mul-
tiply and be useful to others. By remaining in the granary, it becomes food for
rats. A mere scriptural scholar is like the
grain in the granary. How can he make
use of his knowledge without *sadhana*?
Like a parrot, he can just repeat, "I am
Brahman, I am *Brahman*."

The Paths Of Knowledge, Devotion & Action

Equanimity is yoga (union with God). Once one attains that equanimity, Grace flows continuously. No more *sadhana* is needed. One person may like to eat ripe jack fruit raw, another may like it cooked and a third may prefer it roasted. Even though tastes differ, the purpose of eating is to appease hunger. In the same way, each person adopts a different path to know God. Children, whatever path one choses to travel, the goal is the same, God-Realization.

Devotion without awareness of the Goal

cannot lead us to Liberation. It can only be another cause of bondage to man. The jasmine creeper doesn't grow upwards; it only branches out sideways by binding onto other trees.

Knowledge devoid of devotion is like chewing stones.

Devotion rooted in the essential Principle is to take refuge in the One God who manifests as the All, with selfless love, without thinking that there are many Gods. Keeping the goal clearly in mind, one should move forward. If one wants to go to the east, it is useless to travel westwards.

Children, the goal of life is God-Realization. Strive for that! Medicine is
applied to a wound only after it is
cleansed of all dirt. Otherwise, it will
not heal and may get infected. Knowledge is imparted only after the ego is
washed away in the waters of devotion,
for only then will spiritual unfoldment
take place.

Butter will not go rancid if it is melted.
But if it refuses to be melted saying, 'I
am butter,' it will eventually stink. As
long as the ego exists, pride and other
impurities can be melted away only by
devotion. Then the ego no longer stinks.

Some people ask why Mother is giving
importance to the Path of Devotion.
Children, even Sankaracharya, who
established Advaita (philosophy of non-
dualism) at last had to write 'Soundarya

Lahari' (verses glorifying the Divine Mother). Sage Vyasa, the composer of the Brahmasutras, was content only after writing the *Bhagavatam*. One or two out of a thousand may be able to reach the goal through the Path of Knowledge. Can Mother discard the rest of the seekers? Only the Path of Devotion will benefit them. Realizing that talking about Advaita or writing the Brahmasutras was not useful for ordinary people, Sankara and Vyasa composed devotional works.

On the Path of Devotion, we can enjoy the fruit of bliss from the very beginning, whereas on other paths, it can be experienced only toward the end. Bhakti,(devotion), is like the jackfruit tree that bears fruit at its base. One has to climb to the top of other trees to pluck their fruit.

Initially we should have 'bhaya bhakti' (reverence and devotion with an element of fear) toward God. Afterward, when the state of Supreme Love is reached, fear dissolves.

No matter how much we meditate and do *japa*, if we have no love for God, our efforts are fruitless. No matter how hard we row, our boat will only inch its way along if it moves against the current. But if we raise a sail, the boat will pick up speed. Love for God is like the sail which will help us progress fast and reach the Goal quickly.

People may say that performing 'karma' is enough. But to perform 'karma', knowledge is necessary. Action without knowledge will not be right action.

Actions done with *sraddha* (attention and care) will lead us to God. *Sraddha* must be present. Only through *sraddha* can we attain concentration. Often, we consider things we should have taken care of only after the action is done. Only after leaving the examination hall do we think, "Oh, I should have answered another way." What is the use of thinking of it afterwards?

Children, whatever action is performed, *sraddha* is necessary. Action done without *sraddha* is useless. A *sadhak* can recollect the details of actions performed many years ago, because of the extreme attention with which he performed them. Even while doing apparently trivial actions, we should pay attention.

We are very careful when we pick up a needle, even though we consider it an insignificant thing. Without paying attention, we cannot pass the thread through the eye of the needle. If we are inattentive for a moment while sewing, we may pierce our finger with the needle. We never leave a needle lying about carelessly, lest it pierce someone's foot. A *sadhak* must exercise such attention whenever he is doing any work.

One should not talk while working, as talking diminishes concentration. Action performed without attention is useless. Do not forget to do mantra *japa* while doing your work. If you cannot do *japa* and work simultaneously, pray before starting, "God, I am doing Your work. Please give me the strength and ability to perform it. I am working through Your Power."

One who constantly maintains the re-membrance of God while doing any work is the real karma yogi, the true seeker. He sees God in whatever work he does. His mind is not in the work, but rests in God.

Only a very few people who have the samskara inherited from previous births can follow the Path of Knowledge. But if a true Guru is guiding you, you will have no problem on any path.

In meditation with form, we meditate on ourselves only. At midday when the sun is directly overhead, there is no shadow. Meditation with form is like that; when you reach a certain stage, the form of meditation disappears. When the stage of Perfection is reached, there is no shadow, no duality, no illusion.

First external alertness is necessary. When our external behaviour is not alert,we cannot possibly conquer our internal nature.

Pranayama (Breath Control)

Pranayama should be practiced with utmost care. While practicing the exercises, one should sit with the spine erect. Ordinary diseases can be treated and cured, but not the disorders caused by incorrect practice of *pranayama*.

When *pranayama* is practiced, there is movement in the intestine in the lower abdominal area. Pranayamic exercises have a specified duration of time; if this order is violated, the digestive system can be irreparably damaged and the food taken in will pass out undigested. Therefore, *pranayama* must be practiced only under the direct guidance of an adept who knows what should be done at each stage and who gives appropriate herbal medicine, etc. If *pranayama* is practiced relying just on instructions from books, it can be injurious. No one should do it.

Children, the number of times *pranayama* is to be performed is specified for each stage. If that direction is not properly followed, it can be dangerous. The effect will be like trying to stuff a sack of 5 kilo capacity with 10 kilos of rice.

Kumbhaka is the stillness of breath which occurs when concentration is perfected. One might even say that breath itself is thought. The rhythm of breath will change according to the concentration of thoughts.

Even without *pranayama*, kumbhaka (retention of breath) can happen through devotion. Doing *japa* continuously is enough.

Meditation

Making the mind concentrated is real education or knowledge.

One may meditate by fixing the attention on the heart or between the eyebrows. As long as one is unable to sit comfortably in a particular posture, one should meditate by fixing the attention on the heart. Meditation between the eyebrows is to be practiced only in the presence of the Guru because during this meditation, the head may become heated and headache and giddiness may be experienced. Sometimes one may suffer from insomnia. The Guru knows what is to be done on such occasions.

Meditation helps to free the mind from restlessness and tension. To practice meditation, belief in God is not necessary. The mind can be fixed on any part of the body or on any point. One may also imagine that he is merging in the Infinite, just as a river merges in the ocean.

Happiness comes from the dissolution of mind, not from external objects. Through meditation we can achieve everything including bliss, longevity, charm, health, strength, intelligence and vitality. But it should be practiced properly in solitude and with care.

It is possible to gain concentration as well as mental purity by meditating on the forms of God. Even without our being aware of it, the pure (sattvic) qualities of our Beloved Deity will develop within us. Even while sitting idle, do not let your mind wander. Wherever your eyes fall, imagine the form of your Chosen Deity there.

If you like to meditate on a flame, that is enough. Look at the flame of a candle in a dark room for some time. The flame should be steady. You can meditate on this flame in the heart or between the eyebrows. You can also concentrate on the light that appears when your eyes are closed after gazing at the external flame. You can meditate by imagining that the Beloved Deity is standing in the flame, but to meditate on the Beloved Deity standing in the sacrificial fire is even better. Imagine that anger, jealousy, ego, and all negativities are being consumed in the sacrificial fire.

Don't stop meditating just because the

form is not clear. Imagine that you see each part of the Beloved Deity within, beginning with the feet and moving up to the head. Do the ritual bathing of God. Adorn the Deity with robes and ornaments. Feed Him or Her with your own hand. Through these visualizations, the Beloved Deity's form will not fade away from the mind.

Children, to compel the mind to meditate is like trying to submerge a piece of wood in water. If one loosens his grip, the wood pops up immediately. If you cannot meditate, do *japa*. Through *japa* the mind will become amenable to meditation.

Initially meditation on form is necessary. Through this practice, the mind becomes focused on the Beloved Deity. However one meditates and whatever the object of meditation, concentration is essential.

What is the use of affixing superfluous stamps on a letter without writing the address? Doing *japa* and meditation without concentration is like doing that.

When we try to eliminate negative thoughts, they start to cause trouble. When we were previously indulging these thoughts, they were not bothersome. Now we have a different attitude. That is why we have become aware of negative thoughts. Although they were there in our mind previously, we did not notice them. When these thoughts rise in the mind as we meditate, we should discriminate in this way: "Oh mind, is there any use dwelling on these thoughts? Is your goal to think about such things?" Total dispassion must be developed toward worldly objects. Detachment must be cultivated so that love for God may grow.

Children, if you feel sleepy while meditating, you must take special care not to succumb to the enslavement of sleep. In the initial stages of meditation, all tamasic (dull) qualities will surface. If you are vigilant, these will vanish eventually. When you feel sleepy, get up and do *japa* while walking; using the mala (rosary), hold it close to your chest with alertness. In an unhurried manner, continue *japa*. If you still feel sleepy, do *japa* while standing without leaning against anything or moving your legs.

Wherever we may be, sitting or standing, the spine should always be kept straight. Do not meditate with the spine hunched over. The mind is a thief always waiting for an opportunity to enslave us. If we lean on anything, we will sleep without even knowing it.

A minimum of three years is required to learn to fix one's attention firmly on the form of meditation within. Initially one must strive for concentration by looking at a photo. If one meditates with closed eyes for ten minutes, then for ten minutes one should look at the form of meditation. Eventually the form will become clear within.

At night the atmosphere is calm because sleep subdues birds, animals and worldly people. Waves of worldly thoughts diminish during the night. Flowers blossom in the late hours of the night. The atmosphere has a unique energizing effect. If meditation is done at this time, the mind easily becomes one-pointed and remains absorbed in meditation for a long time. Night is the time when yogis remain awake.

Mantra

If mantras have no power, words have no power. If one angrily orders a person, "Get out!" one causes an entirely different effect than if one kindly asks him, "Please leave." Are different reactions not created in the listener?

Mantra is for making our mind pure, not to satisfy God, for what is the mantra to God?

Don't trouble the intellect by pondering the meaning of the mantra; it is enough to chant the mantra. You may have come to the Ashram by bus, car, boat or train, but do you waste your time thinking about the vehicle? It is enough that one becomes aware of the Goal.

There are various types of diksha (initiation): diksha by glance, by touch, by thought, by mantra, etc. There is no harm in giving the mantra in writing. Once a mantra is given in initiation, the disciple's whole burden is shifted onto the Guru. Mantra upadesa should be obtained from a Satguru (Realised Master). If the Guru is not a Satguru, the result resembles using a dirty filter to purify water; the water will become more impure.

Children, even though you have boarded the bus and purchased the ticket, don't be careless. Keep the ticket safe. If we don't show our ticket when the ticket checker comes, he will put us off. In the same way just because you have been given a mantra, don't think that your responsibility ends there. Only if you use a mantra properly will it take you to the goal.

Japa & Bhajan

Children, it is difficult to row a boat through water covered with water plants. If one first removes them, the boat will move with greater ease. Similarly, if the mind's impurities are eliminated by *japa*, meditation will be easier.

Continuous *japa* without *sraddha* is as harmful as the incorrect practice of *pranayama*. During *japa*, try to avoid other thoughts as vigilantly as possible. Fix the mind either on the form of meditation or on the letters of the mantra.

Children, always chant the mantra. The mind must be trained to do *japa* incessantly. Then whatever work we may do, the mind will continue *japa*. A spider continues to spin a web wherever it goes. In the same way, during every action, continue *japa* mentally.

If the form fades away during meditation, imagine the form again. Also imagine coiling the rope of *japa* around the Beloved Deity from foot to head and then uncoiling the rope. This will help fix the mind on the Deity.

No matter how much we feed a cat and caress it, the moment we divert our attention, it will steal things. The mind is also like this. To tame and concentrate the mind, always repeat the mantra while walking, sitting, working. The mantra should continue like the flow of oil being poured from one vessel to another.

In the initial stages of *sadhana*, along with contemplation of form, *japa* is also necessary. Don't worry if the form is not clear; it is enough to continue *japa*. As you make progress in *sadhana*, the mind will become fixed on the form and *japa* will naturally slow down.

In *Kaliyuga* (the dark age of materialism), *bhajan* (devotional singing) and *japa* are effective. The money gained by selling a thousand acres of land in former times can be earned by selling one acre of land today. This is the special characteristic of *Kaliyuga*. Even five minutes of concentration gained is a great asset.

Children, it is not necessary to chant the different *Sahasranamas* (the Thousand Names of God). Any one of them is enough. Everything is contained in each *Sahasranama*.

At dusk, the atmosphere is full of impure vibrations. This is the time when day and night meet and is the best time for *sadhaks* to meditate because good concentration can be attained. If *sadhana* is not done, more worldly thoughts rise up. That is why *bhajan* should be sung loudly at dusk. In this way, the atmosphere will also be purified.

Children, at dusk sing *bhajan* while sitting in front of a burning oil lamp. The smoke produced by the wick burning in oil is a *siddha oushada* (perfect medicine). We inhale the smoke and the atmosphere is also purified.

Since the atmosphere in *Kaliyuga* is full of sounds, *bhajan* is better than meditation for obtaining concentration. For meditation, quiet surroundings are necessary. For this reason, *bhajan* is more effective to gain concentration. By loud singing one can overcome other distracting sounds and achieve concentration. Concentration precedes meditation. *Bhajan*, concentration, meditation; this is the progression. Children, constant remembrance of God is meditation.

Without concentration, singing *bhajan* is only a waste of energy. If one sings *bhajan* with one-pointedness, one will benefit oneself, the listener and Nature as well. Devotional songs help to awaken the mind of the listener.

Children, whenever the mind is restless, do mantra *japa*; otherwise, the restlessness will only increase. When devoid of calmness, the mind will seek external objects. If one object does not satisfy it, the mind will turn to something else. External objects cannot give us tranquillity; only remembrance of God and mantra *japa* can restore quietude to the mind. Reading spiritual books also helps.

Children learn to count by using an abacus. By this method they learn quickly. To keep the mind under control, a mala is useful. Later *japa* can be done without a mala. If we do *japa* continually, it will become part of our character. Even while we sleep, *japa* will continue without our knowledge.

Observance Of Vows

Children, the shore checks the waves of the sea. In spiritual life, the observance of vows controls the waves of the mind.

On certain days (ekadasi, full moon, etc.), the atmosphere is completely impure. At these times, to observe a vow of silence and eat only fruit is a good practice. Since fruit is covered by peel, atmospheric impurities do not affect it very much. These days are favorable for *sadhana.* Whatever thought we may have, spiritual or worldly, more concentration can be attained on these days.

It is good for a seeker to purge the stomach at least twice a month. Once a week, with a vow of silence and a diet of fruit, devote the day to *dhyana* and *japa*. This will be beneficial for the body and *sadhana*.

A seeker who does regular *sadhana* can make his mind and body fit for meditation by observing a fast. Those who meditate and do other work side by side should never fast. They should take the required quantity of food; fruits are very good.

The effect of talking right after meditation is like spending all one's hard-earned money to buy peanuts. The power acquired through meditation will be completely exhausted.

A seeker should utter every word carefully. He should speak sparingly and in a subdued tone so that the listener will hear only when his mind and sense organs are very attentive.

A sick person should observe restrictions in order to be cured. A seeker should also accept restrictions until he reaches the Goal. Minimal conversation, a vow of silence, controlled diet, are the restrictions.

To observe vows is not a weakness. Wooden planks are useful in building a boat only if they can be bent. In order to bend them, the shipwright heats them. Likewise, by observing spiritual discipline, the *sadhak* can bring his mind under control. Without taming the mind, the body cannot be controlled.

Patience & Discipline

Children, spiritual life is possible only for one who has patience.

It is not possible to measure one's spiritual growth by observing external actions. However, spiritual advancement can be understood to some degree by observing one's reactions to adverse circumstances.

How can a person who gets angry over a petty thing lead the world? Children, only a person with patience can guide people. Ego must be completely annihilated. No matter how many people sit in a chair, it does not complain. In the same way, no matter how many people get angry with us, we should develop the strength to endure and forgive. Otherwise, performing *sadhana* is of no use.

Through anger much of the power gained by *sadhana* can be lost. While a vehicle is running, not much energy is dissipated, but to stop it and then start it again takes more fuel. In the same way, power is drained through every pore of the body when one gets angry.

When a cigarette lighter is pressed ten or twenty times, the fuel is spent. One knows this without seeing it. Similarly, the energy acquired through good thoughts can be lost in many ways. For instance, when we get angry, whatever we have gained through *sadhana* is lost.

When we talk, energy is spent only through the mouth, but anger dissipates energy through the eyes and ears as well as through each pore of the body.

Children, keeping a strict timetable is vital for a spiritual aspirant. A daily routine of *japa* and meditation should be observed at the same time and for a set duration. The habit of meditating every day at a fixed time should be developed. This habit will guide us.

Those who have a regular timetable of spiritual discipline follow it at the fixed time automatically. One who has grown accustomed to drinking tea at a particular time wants tea at that time; otherwise he becomes restless and runs for tea.

Humility

Huge trees are uprooted and buildings collapse in a cyclone, but no matter how strong a cyclone is, it cannot touch the grass. This is the greatness of humility.

To bow down to others is not weakness. We should have the greatness to bow down even to the grass. If a person decides to take a bath but is not ready to bow down to the river, his body will remain dirty. By saying that he will not bow down to others, a *sadhak* is not allowing his ignorance to be destroyed.

Man egotistically claims that by merely pressing a button he can burn the world to ashes. In order to press the button his hand must move. He does not think about the Power behind this movement.

Men say they have conquered the world. They do not even have the ability to count the grains of sand under their feet. Such small fries say they have conquered the world.

Suppose someone gets angry with you for no reason. Even then a *sadhak* should have the humility to bow down to him, realizing that this is a play of God in order to test him. Only then has the benefit of meditation been attained.

Children, even when a man is cutting a tree down from its very root, it gives him shade. A spiritual aspirant should be like the tree. Only he who prays even for the welfare of those who torment him can become a spiritual person.

Selfishness & Desire

Children, ego arises out of desire and selfishness; it does not occur naturally but is created.

Suppose we intend to collect some money. We expect to receive two hundred rupees, but receive only fifty rupees. We get so angry that we pounce on the debtor and beat him up. The matter then becomes a court case. Does our anger not result from being denied the desired amount? What is the use of blaming God when we receive the punishment which our action has brought upon us? Anger arises from expectation; sorrow arises from desire. Painful consequences result from running after desires.

The wind of God's Grace cannot lift us if we are carrying the load of desires and ego; the load should be reduced.

Many flowers bloom on a tree which sheds all its leaves; on other trees flowers bloom only here and there. Children, when we are totally free from negative tendencies such as selfishness, ego and jealousy, we will attain the Vision of God.

A *sadhak* should not have even a trace of selfishness. Selfishness is like a worm that sucks the honey from flowers. If worms are allowed to grow, the fruit becomes infested. There is no use for such fruit. In the same way, if selfishness is allowed to grow, it will gnaw away all our good qualities.

Children, there is a great difference between the desires of a *sadhak* and those of a worldly person. Like waves, desires come one after another to disturb the worldly man. His desires have no end. For a spiritual seeker there is only one desire; once it is fulfilled, desire is no more.

The selfishness of a spiritual aspirant is beneficial to the world. Once there were two boys in a village. Both of them received a seed from a wandering sannysi. The first boy roasted the seed and ate it, appeasing his hunger; he was a worldly person. The second boy sowed the seed producing much grain, which he then distributed to others. Children, even though both boys had the selfishness to acquire the seed, the selfishness of the second boy was beneficial to many people.

There is only one *Atman*. It is all-pervasive. When our minds become expansive, we will merge with It. Then selfishness and ego will vanish. Everything is equal. Children, without wasting a single moment, serve others, especially destitute people. Without expecting anything from others, serve them freely.

Small selfishness can get rid of big selfishness. A small notice, 'Stick No Bills', will keep the rest of the wall clean. Selfishness for God is like that.

Food

Without forsaking the taste of the tongue, one cannot enjoy the taste of the heart.

It is not possible to state definitely, 'Eat this; do not eat that.' The influence of our diet on us changes according to climatic conditions. The types of food we avoid here may be useful in the Himalayas.

When we sit down to eat our food, we must first pray to God. This is why we chant a mantra before eating. The proper time to test our patience is when food is before us.

An ascetic need not wander in search of food. The spider weaves its web and remains where it is. It does not go anywhere searching for food; its prey will get entangled in its web. In the same way, an ascetic's food will come to him from God, but he must be a man of total surrender.

Diet has a great deal of influence on our character. Stale foods will increase our *tamas* (sluggishness).

In the initial stages a *sadhak* should exercise control regarding food. An uncontrolled diet produces bad tendencies. When seeds are newly sown, one must protect them from crows. After a seed has grown into a tree, any bird can sit on it or build a nest in it. In the beginning, diet must be controlled and *sadhana* performed. At a later stage, hot, sour or non-vegetarian food can be eaten without adverse effect. Children, just because Mother tells you that at a later stage any food can be eaten, don't consume these foods even then. You should live as a model to the world; then others will learn by observing you. Don't use substances which are hot and sour in front of a person affected by jaundice. Even though we don't have the disease ourselves, we should have self-control in order to set a good example for others.

One may say that to stop drinking tea or to quit smoking is easy, yet one cannot do it. How can someone control his mind if he cannot even control these simple things? First these simple things must be curtailed. If one cannot cross small rivers, how can one cross the ocean?

In the beginning, a *sadhak* should not eat anything from shops. While measuring each ingredient, the shopkeeper thinks, "Do I need to use this much milk? Why not reduce the sugar?" In this way, he thinks only of reducing the quantity to earn profit. The vibration of these thoughts affects the *sadhak*.

Once a *sannyasi*, who did not read newspapers, became aware of having an intense desire to read the newspaper. Then he started dreaming about newspapers and the news. When he inquired, he discovered that the servant was reading the newspaper while cooking. His attention was not on the cooking but on reading the newspaper. The thought waves of the cook affected the *sannyasi*.

Don't stuff yourself. Fill only half the stomach with food, a quarter with water and leave the remaining space for the movement of air. The less food you eat, the more mental control you will have. Do not sleep or meditate imme-diately after eating; otherwise, proper digestion will not take place.

Once we develop love of God, we are like a man suffering from fever. We will not find any taste in food. Even though the food be sweet, it will taste bitter to us. Once we love God, our appetite spontaneously decreases.

Brahmacharya (Celibacy)

Children, hot and sour foods are harmful to *brahmacharya*. Too much salt should be avoided, but sweet food to a certain extent is harmless. It is not wise to consume curd (yogurt) at night, or to use too much milk. Milk for drinking should be mixed with an equal amount of water and then boiled. Too much oil should be avoided or there will be an increase in the fat content of the body, which creates an increase in semen as well.

One should not eat tasty food frequently. If the desire for tasty food increases, temptations of the body also increase. Not to take food in the morning is best, and only a small quantity should be taken at night.

One need not be afraid of the emission of semen during sleep. Haven't you seen cow dung being burnt and mixed with water to make sacred ash? A cloth wick is placed inside the vessel with one end hanging out. Excess water oozes out through this wick, but the essence is not lost. Sacred ash precipitates only after the water is expelled. But take special care that emission does not occur while dreaming.

Children, whenever you feel that emission is about to occur, get up immediately and do meditation or *japa*. Whether it happens or not, observe a fast the next day while performing your *sadhana*. Bathing in a river or in the sea is good for *brahmacharya*.

During certain months and days the atmosphere is completely impure. At these times, however much care you take, emission may occur. Mid-July to mid-August is such a time.

Due to heat generated by the mind's concentration, the power of *brahmacharya* is transformed into *ojas* (sublimated vital force). If a worldly man observes celibacy, he should perform *sadhana* as well, or the power of *brahmacharya* will not be converted into *ojas*.

Sadhak & Sadhana

Children, our attitude toward each object in Creation should be free from any expectation. *Sadhana* develops this attitude.

There is no shortcut to the Vision of God. Though sugar candy is sweet, nobody swallows it all at once lest it scratch his throat. He dissolves it and swallows it slowly. Similarly, one must perform *sadhana* regularly and patiently.

Without love of God doing *japa* or meditation is of no use. But those who think that they can wait to begin *sadhana* while developing love of God are idlers. They are like those who wait for the waves of the ocean to subside before bathing.

Through *sadhana* we are filled with *shakti* (energy) and the body is freed from diseases. Then we can perform any action without collapsing.

Through *sadhana* the Deity takes us to the threshold. If one travels fifty kilometers by bus to the Ashram at Vallickavu, one can easily walk the remaining kilometer. The Deity brings us to the gate of *Akhanda Satchidananda* (Undivided Existence-Awareness-Bliss).

Children, before we set out to teach the world, we should gain the strength to do so. Those who go to the Himalayas take woolen clothing to protect them from the cold. In the same way, our mind must be strengthened before we enter the world, so as not to be disturbed by adversity. This is possible only through *sadhana.*

Real *satsang* is the union of the individual self with the Supreme Self.

If one has a craving for dates, one will risk climbing through even a wasp-infested tree in order to reach them. Similarly, one who has *lakshya bodha* (intent to reach the Goal) will overcome any adverse circumstances.

In the beginning, going on a pilgrimage is beneficial for a *sadhak*. A journey with hardships will help him understand the nature of the world. One who has not gained strength through *sadhana* will break down under the duress of conditions in the world. Therefore, continuous *sadhana* is essential, staying in one place and wasting no time.

The perfection of *asana* (sitting posture) is the first thing a *sadhak* must master. This is not always easy to achieve. Each day sit five minutes more than you did the previous day. In this way, you will gradually be able to sit for two or three hours at a stretch. When you acquire patience, then everything will come easily.

Children, crying to God for five minutes is equal to an hour of meditation. When crying, the mind easily becomes absorbed in the remembrance of God. If you cannot cry, pray, "O God, why am I unable to cry to You?"

A spiritual aspirant should not cry for ephemeral things; he must cry only for Truth. Shed tears only for God. A spiritual aspirant must never become weak. He has to shoulder the burden of the whole world.

Our attitude can be expressed in three ways: through words, through tears, through laughter. Children, only when mental impurities are washed away by tears can we smile with an open heart. Then true happiness will dawn.

Sadhana is essential. Even though the seed contains the plant, it will only bear fruit when it is properly cultivated and given fertilizer. In the same way, even though Supreme Truth resides in all living beings, it will shine only through *sadhana*.

If one does not properly care for a plant after planting it, it will dry up. One must give it constant attention. Then the plant will not be harmed; even if the top of it is cut off, it will grow many new branches. However difficult the rules may be, a *sadhak* must follow them in the beginning stages. Only then will he grow.

A spiritual aspirant should visit slums, hospitals, and orphanages at least once a month. These visits will help him understand the nature of life's miseries and make his mind strong and compassionate.

Do not disturb milk which is set for curd. Only if it is allowed to set will it become curd. In the beginning stages of *sadhana*, solitude is necessary.

When one sows seeds, he takes care that chickens do not feed on them. After the seeds sprout, there is no problem. In the beginning, a seeker should not be attached to anyone. Devotees leading a household life should be especially careful of this. Waste no time chatting with the neighbors; whenever you have time, sit for *japa*, *bhajan* or meditation.

There are no waves in the deep sea. There are waves only in shallow areas near the shoreline. Those who have attained Perfection are calm. People with little knowledge create problems after reading two or three books.

The waves of the sea cannot be destroyed; the thoughts of the mind cannot be eliminated. Once the mind gains depth and breadth, thought waves will subside naturally.

Children, both the real and the unreal are contained in a seed. When a seed is sown, the husk cracks and becomes one with the soil. The essence of the seed sprouts and grows. Similarly, both real and unreal are within us. If we live holding to the real, nothing will bother us; we will become expansive. If we resort to the unreal, we cannot grow.

For one who knows Reality, the whole world is his wealth. He cannot see anything as different from his own Self.

It is through one's deeds that one's worth is determined. Even though one may be well educated and employed, if he steals, no one will respect him. A sadhak's progress should be judged by his deeds.

Wherever a *sadhak* may stand, sit or lie down, he should be perfectly still with no unnecessary movement of the hands, legs or body. He should imagine that the body is dead. Eventually, through practice, stillness will become a habit. Have you not seen soldiers and policemen standing like statues even in the rain and hot sun?

A man who takes a boat into the sea beyond the waves rows the boat with closed eyes. People standing on the shore encourage him by waving their arms and shouting. The man rowing does not pay any attention to them. His only thought is to get the boat beyond the grip of the waves. Once he crosses the waves, he has nothing to fear. If he wishes, he can even rest on the oars for a few minutes. You, too, are crossing the waves. Without paying attention to other things, proceed vigilantly; keep the goal before you and you will reach the destination.

A spiritual aspirant should be very careful relating to members of the opposite sex. You realize the danger of a whirlwind only after it seizes you and flings you down.

Children, water has no colour, but a lake or pond reflects the colour of the sky. We see bad qualities in others only because we ourselves have faults in our character. Always try to see good in others.

A *sadhak* should not take part in ceremonies surrounding marriage or death.

Whether young or old, everyone at a wedding thinks of the pleasures of marriage; at rituals for the dead, people grieve over the loss of a mortal being. The thought waves of both are harmful to a seeker. These vibrations enter the subconscious mind and make one restless for unreal things.

A spiritual person should be like the wind. The wind blows over fragrant flowers as well as foul-smelling excreta without bias. Like the wind, a *sadhak* should have neither attachment to people who show him affection nor malice toward those who abuse him. To him everyone is equal. He should see God in everything.

Fruit which appears ripe externally will soon decay. Fruit which ripens from the inside will last. Introversion is necessary. Without help from outside, we learn to enjoy happiness from within. We only have problems when we seek happiness in external objects.

It is not good to sleep during the daytime; when we wake up, we feel exhausted. This is because during the daytime the atmosphere is full of impure thought waves. When we get up in the morning after a night's sleep we feel energetic, because the atmosphere is far less polluted at night. That is why *sadhaks* meditate during the night. Meditate for five hours at night rather than ten hours during the day.

While walking, sitting, or bathing, imagine that the Beloved Deity is walking beside you, smiling at you. Imagine the Beloved Deity standing in the sky and cry to Him or Her. Children, whatever grievances you may have, look at Nature and imagine the Beloved Deity's form in the trees, the mountains and other objects. Converse with them. Imagine that the Beloved Deity is standing in the sky and call to Him or Her. Why should you tell your sorrows to others?

If we stand near someone who is talking, that talk creates a particular aura around us. If we keep bad company, a negative aura forms causing an increase of impure thoughts in us. That is why *satsang* (keeping holy company) is necessary.

When a sculptor looks at a piece of wood or stone, he sees only the image that can be carved or sculpted; others see only rock or wood. Similarly, a seeker should discriminate between what is eternal and what is ephemeral and live with vigilant attention. He must hold on to the eternal alone. The eternal is God; worldly matters are transitory.

Children, we are not sexually tempted by the nudity of a child. We should be able to look at anyone in the same spirit. Everything depends on the mind.

A *sadhak* should be conscientious in the beginning of his *sadhana*. The favorable time for meditation is in the morning before eleven o'clock and after five o'clock in the evening. Immediately after meditation, one should lie down in *savasana* (corpse pose) for at least ten minutes. Even if one meditates for only an hour, one should remain silent for at least half an hour afterward. Only those who do this receive the full benefit of meditation.

After medicine is injected, it takes some time before it spreads throughout the body. In the same way, after doing spiritual practices, one should spend some time in silence. If one starts talking of worldly things after two hours of meditation, even five years of meditation will be useless.

If someone talks about unnecessary things and wastes our time, we should either repeat our mantra silently or contemplate the Beloved Deity. Imagine that the person talking is the Beloved Deity, or draw a triangle on the ground imagining your Deity standing in it. Take small stones and, thinking of them as flowers, offer them at the Feet of your Beloved Deity. Discuss only spiritual matters with others. Those who have affinity for spiritual subjects will listen; others will leave immediately. No time will be lost.

Children, even the breath of a *sadhak* is enough to purify the atmosphere; it has great power. Scientists will discover this eventually. Only then will people believe it completely.

Human beings are not the only ones with the capacity for speech. Animals, birds and plants also have the power to communicate, but we don't have the ability to understand them. One who has the Vision of the Self knows all these things.

Sadhak & Relatives

Children, if no one can look after the parents of a family, a son has the responsibility to care for them, even though he may have chosen the spiritual path. One should see one's parents as one's own self and serve them accordingly.

If one's parents pose a hindrance to spiritual life, one need not obey them.

What is the use of taking up spiritual life if one disobeys his parents? Suppose one has to go to a distant place to study medicine, but his parents do not approve. If the son disobeys, goes to study and becomes a doctor, he can save thousands of people from death, including his parents. His disobedience becomes a benefit to the world; he is harming no one. If he had obeyed his parents and not studied, he could only look after them but not save them from suffering and death. It is possible only for a spiritual seeker to love his parents and the world selflessly and to save them. Did Sankaracharya and Ramana Marharshi not come to their mothers' rescue?

Once one chooses the spiritual path, he must give up attachment to family and relatives; otherwise, he will not be able to progress. If a boat is anchored, one will row in vain; the boat will not move forward. You have dedicated your lives to God; you must have strong faith that He will look after your family.

Children, who are our true mother and father? Are they our birth parents? No. They are only our stepmother and stepfather. The true mother or father is the one capable of bringing a dying man back to life; only God has that power. Always remember this.

Small plants which grow in the shade of big trees grow comfortably for some time, but when the tree sheds its leaves, they wither away in the sun. Those who grow in the shade of relatives are like these plants.

To Householders

Today everybody's love and devotion to God is like love for the neighbours; when our neighbours do not give us what we want, we fight with them. With God we do the same thing; we abandon *japa* and our prayers.

How hard we work to win a case in court! Just to get a ticket for the cinema we are willing to endure pushing and shoving. We willingly tolerate these troubles for the sake of some external happiness. If we made such sacrifices for spiritual life, we would soon enjoy Eternal Bliss.

Suppose a child cuts his hand. If we say, "You are not the body, nor the mind or intellect," he will not understand and will only cry. Likewise, it is no use telling a worldly man, "You are not the body, you are *Brahman* (Supreme Reality). The world is unreal." Perhaps some change can be brought about, but instead we should tell him things that he can use in daily life.

Children, those who take sudden delight in spirituality upon hearing spiritual discourses will not be able to lead a stable spiritual life. However long one may squeeze a spring, it will immediately resume its original shape when the pressure is released.

Nowadays it seems that nobody has time to go to temples or ashrams or to do *sadhana*. But if our child is sick, we are willing to wait without sleep for any length of time in the hospital waiting room. For a square foot of land we ignore our family and gladly wait in front of the courthouse for any number of days in the rain or sun. We have time to linger for hours in a shop simply to purchase a packet of needles for fifty cents. But we have no time to pray to God. Children, when we love God, we will easily find time for our *sadhana*.

Who has no time to do *japa*? One can say a mantra every so many steps. Can't one do *japa* while travelling in a bus by imagining the Beloved Deity's form in the sky, or recite the mantra with eyes closed? If one does *japa* this way, one loses no time allowing the mind to get entangled in roadside attractions. It is surely possible to do *japa* while performing household duties. Those whose hearts seek God will always have time for spiritual practices.

When people cannot sleep, they take sleeping pills. When they seek escape from sorrow, they go to movies or consume intoxicants like liquor and ganja, which are readily available. Because these things dull their senses, nobody is searching for God these days. People do not know that these intoxicants are destroying them. When one consumes intoxicants, the water content is reduced in the brain. It is then that one feels intoxicated. Through continuous use of these substances, the nerves in the body start to contract due to dehydration. After some time, affected by shaking and tiredness, one has difficulty even walking. Losing vitality and brilliance, the person will degenerate, and his children, too, will be affected by the same condition.

Children, it is the mind that needs to be air-conditioned, not the room. People air-condition their room and still they commit suicide there. Would they do this if luxury items had given them happiness? True happiness cannot be gained from external things.

When a dog chews a bone, blood oozes, and the dog thinks it is coming from the bone, when it is actually coming from its own injured gums. In this way, we seek happiness from external things, forgetting that true happiness lies only within us.

We do not make a fence by cutting off the branches of a high-yielding fruit tree; we use only branches from useless trees for this purpose. If we understood the value of life, we would not waste it on sensual pleasures.

There is no particular time when a house-holder should begin spiritual life. When he feels the impulse, he should begin. He need not try to create this desire; the urge will come of its own accord. When a hen incubates an egg, she does not peck it open, but waits till the chick hatches of its own accord. If his wife and children can live comfortably, and if he has the spirit of detachment, then he can begin. Once he undertakes spiritual life, he should have no further thought of his home.

In former times people used to teach children what is permanent and what is im-permanent. They taught that the aim of life is God-Realization. Children were given training which enabled them to know who they were. Now parents en-courage children to be educated only to earn money. The result is that the father does not care for his son and the son does not care for his father. Enmity and fighting are common among them. People even kill others for selfish motives.

Children, without *sadhana* God-Realization is not possible, but nobody is ready to strive for it. Factory workers on the night shift do their job without sleeping. They are not careless just because they are tired. If they are not very alert, they will lose a hand or an arm and their job as well. In spiritual life also this alertness and dispassion are essential.

Small children may worry that the sun has disappeared at sunset. In the morning when it rises, they rejoice at its return. They don't know what the truth is. We rejoice and grieve like them with gain and loss.

In Kerala we can see a man in a tiny boat leading ducks through the backwaters. The boat is so small that he can hardly stretch his legs or breathe deeply without tipping it. Standing in the boat, slapping the oar on the water, the man guides the ducks if they stray. He scoops out any water in the boat with his feet. He also chats with people standing on the bank. Occasionally he smokes. Even though he is doing all these things, his mind is always focused on the oar. If his attention wavers even for a moment, the boat will capsize and he will tumble into the water. Children, we should live in the world with similar vigilance. Whatever work we are doing, our mind should be centered on God.

The folk dancer with a pot on his head does so many tricks. He dances and rolls on the ground, but the pot never slips. His mind is always fixed on the pot. Just so, with practice you can learn to fix the mind on God while doing any work.

Pray to God by crying in solitude. If the body is wounded, the mind is obsessed with the wound. Similarly, we are afflicted with bhavaroga, the disease of transmigration: birth, death and rebirth. If you are earnest about curing the disease, your prayers will be sincere. The heart will melt with love for God.

Brahma, Vishnu and Shiva create, nourish and destroy desires respectively. Man creates and nourishes desires but does not destroy them. Children, destruction of desire is what is needed.

Those who work in offices and banks

handle millions of rupees, but they know that the money does not belong to them. They also know that the customers and clients are not their relatives. They are sure that a client's show of friendliness to them comes from selfishness, therefore they are not concerned whether the client talks to them or not. We, too, should live like this. If we understand that nothing in the world is related to us, then we will have no trouble.

When we are aware of the Goal, concentration will come. We will benefit only through concentration.

The mango seed is bitter, but if it is cooked properly, we can, with effort, make many different dishes from it. The *Srimad Bhagavatam* (holy book of Sri Krishna's life, deeds and teachings) is for seekers. If we read it attentively, we can find all spiritual principles in it. For those who don't have an inquiring mind, it is only a story. Reading the *Bhagavatam* aloud in order to earn money is not right. But if a householder cannot make both ends meet, then he may read it for money.

To live comfortably in a place, you must first clean it thoroughly, removing any garbage from the grounds. Only in clean surroundings will you be able to do *japa* and meditation. If the place is not clean, the smell of garbage will make you restless. *Homas* and *yagas* (sacrifices) are conducted for purification of the atmosphere. By performing them we get fresh air; God does not require *homas* and *yagas*.

In the name of politics people spend huge amounts of money and even commit murder. Millions of rupees were spent for a handful of rocks from the moon, but we have no money to conduct *homas* and *yagas*. Failing to perform these holy sacrifices is understandable, but to condemn them without comprehending their benefit is ludicrous. This is ignorance.

Children, both worldly and spiritual life can be led side by side, but we must act without attachment and expectation. We feel sorrow when we think, "I have done this; I want to reap the fruit of it." Never feel that someone is "your " wife, "your" child, etc. If we think that everything is God's, then we have no attachment. When we die, our wife and child will not accompany us. God is the only Truth.

No matter how much wealth we have, unless we properly understand its value and use, we will experience only sorrow. Even If we have unlimited wealth, the pleasure we derive from it is only temporary. It cannot give eternal happiness. Kings like Kamsa and Hiranyakasipu possesed huge wealth, yet in spite of it, what peace of mind did they have? They strayed from the Path of Truth and lived arrogantly. By doing many prohibited things, they lost quietude and peace.

Mother does not say that one should discard wealth. If we understand how to use wealth properly, we will enjoy the wealth of happiness and peace. Children, for those who are fully devoted to God, wealth is like rice with sand in it.

Freedom From Sorrow

The fruit of any action can be countered by another action. If a stone is thrown upwards, can't it be caught before it falls to the ground? In the same way, the result of any action can be changed in its course. There is no need to grieve and brood over fate. A horoscope can be altered by God's resolve. One may have a strong probability of marriage in one's horoscope, but if one does *sadhana* and keeps *satsang* from an early age, the prospect in the horoscope will change. Even in the epics there are examples of this.

One who is travelling on a river does not bother his head thinking of its origin.

In the past we may have made many mistakes. It is useless to worry about those things now. Strive to shape the future; that is what you must do.

However decayed a potato may be, a sprout will grow from a small part which remains unspoiled. Similarly, if we have even a trace of spiritual affinity in us, we can grow by holding onto it. Never think, "I am a sinner. I am not capable of anything."

All along we have been thinking that the body is real. This has caused us sorrow. Now let us think the opposite way. The *Atman* (Self or Soul) is real and eternal and it is the *Atman* that we seek to realize. If that thought becomes firmly fixed in our consciousness, our sorrows will vanish and we will experience only bliss.

If a person is carrying a heavy load, the mere thought that the resting place is nearby eases his burden, as he can soon unload it there. On the other hand, if he thinks that the resting place is far away, the burden becomes heavier. Similarly, when we think that God is with us, all our burdens become lighter. Once we have climbed into a boat or a bus, why continue to carry the luggage? Put it down! In the same way, dedicate everything to God; He will protect us.

Wherever we go, we find faults and defects in others. Our mind becomes restless because of this habit; we must change it. Forgetting the shortcomings of others, we should look for the good qualities in them and respect them. This is what we need to do. Always see only the good side of everyone; then your sorrow will come to an end.

Suppose we fall into a hole. Do we poke our eyes out because they did not guide us properly? Just as we endure the defects of our eyes, we should put up with others' shortcomings and be kind to them.

Vasanas
(Innate Tendencies)

If we find even a single ant in the sugar, we remove it; otherwise, more ants will follow. In a similar way, even a small trace of selfishness is enough for other *vasanas* to follow.

Exhaustion of *vasanas* and destruction of mind; both are the same. That is Liberation.

The first *vasana* in a *jiva* is derived from God and karma develops from it. From karma flow subsequent births. The wheel goes on revolving. Only through exhaustion of *vasanas* can one escape the endless cycle. Spiritual activities like *satsang*, *bhajan*, and *dhyana* help exhaust *vasanas*.

Vasanas will remain until the attainment of Liberation (*Jivanmukti*). The *vasanas* will be completely eliminated only in the state of *Jivanmukti*. Until we reach that state, we must proceed with utmost discrimination. If we fail to exercise vigilance, we may fall at any moment. Those who drive vehicles on busy roads must be very careful. If they let their eyes wander even for a second, they will cause an accident. When driving over open ground, we have nothing to fear, as no obstacles impede the driver and the vehicle. In the beginning of spiritual life dangers lie all around us; we must exercise utmost care. In the *Jivanmukti* State, only the Pure Self remains. There is no duality and thus there is no danger.

The *vasanas* of a *Jivanmukta* are not *vasanas* in the real sense. Their anger, for instance, is only an external show. They are very pure within. Quicklime (calcium carbonate) gives the appearance of having form, but if we touch it, it crumbles.

Children, only the Guru can completely remove our *vasanas*. Unless one is born with powerful spiritual tendencies, there is no other way. The jackal may think, "I will not howl anymore when I see a dog," but the moment it sees a dog, it howls as it always has. It is the same with *vasanas*.

It is not easy to eliminate the flow of thoughts; the disappearance of thoughts is an advanced state. However, by increasing pure thoughts, impure thoughts can be diminished and destroyed.

If we have salt water in a container and add pure water to it again and again, the water will lose its saltiness. In a similar way, bad *vasanas* can be gradually eliminated by good thoughts.

Siddhis (Psychic Powers)

Children, the display of *siddhis* beyond a certain limit violates nature. People are attracted by the display of *siddhis*. As much as possible, a Realized Soul avoids manifesting *siddhis*. Even if he displays any *siddhis*, he loses no energy. If the power of revealing a *siddhi* is used instead to change a man into a *sannyasi*, that will benefit the world. If one becomes fascinated with *siddhis*, he will swerve from his goal.

Realized Souls do not generally show *siddhis*. They may show them only rarely, if at all. Their *siddhis* arise spontaneously in particular circumstances and are not for entertaining onlookers. Don't run after *siddhis*; they are impermanent. Incarnations come to remove desires, not to create them.

Samadhi

Children, sahaja *samadhi* (natural abidance in the Self) is Perfection. One who is established in this state sees the Divine Principle in everything. Everywhere he perceives only Pure Consciousness, free from the taint of *Maya*. Just as a sculptor sees in a stone only the image that can be chiselled from it, Great Souls see only the all-pervading Divinity in everything.

Imagine that there is a rubber ball and a ring within us. The ball is always bouncing up and down; this is our mind, and the ring is our goal. Sometimes the ball gets caught in the ring and remains motionless. This can be called *samadhi*. But the ball does not rest there permanently, it bounces up and down again as before.

Eventually, a state is reached when the ball rests permanently in the ring without any further motion. This is called sahaja *samadhi*.

By meditating on a form, savikalpa *samadhi* (perception of the Real while retaining the sense of duality) can be attained. When one sees the form of the Beloved Deity, the attitude of "I" remains, and therefore duality. In formless meditation, since there is no trace of "I-ness", the attitude of duality is completely destroyed. Nirvikalpa *samadhi* is attained in this way.

In the state of nirvikalpa *samadhi*, there is no entity to say, "I am *Brahman*." One is merged with *Brahman*. If an ordinary man attains nirvikalpa *samadhi*, he casts off his body. He becomes absorbed in *samadhi* quickly, since he has no thought of action to be performed later. When a soda bottle is opened, the gas becomes one with the air outside with a sound. Like this, he becomes one with *Brahman* forever. Only Incarnations can sustain their bodies after attaining nirvikalpa *samadhi*. Knowing the purpose of their incarnation and by maintaining their resolve, they descend to the world again.

Children, for Incarnations there are no distinctions like nirvikalpa *samadhi* or the state above or below it. Incarnations have only a few limitations which they themselves have assumed in order to accomplish the purpose for which they have incarnated themselves.

Even after attaining nirvikalpa *samadhi*, a *sadhak* who attained it through *sadhana* does not become equal to an Incarnation. The difference is like that of a man who has visited Bombay and one who lives there. If one asks them whether they have ever been to Bombay, both will say "yes", but the one who lives there permanently has a thorough knowledge of the city and its byways.

What will *samadhi* be like? Bliss. No happiness, no sorrow. No "I" and no "you". This state can be compared to deep sleep, but there is a vast difference. In *samadhi* there is full awareness. Only when we wake up, you, I and the world emerge. We only give reality to them because of our ignorance.

It is not possible to describe the experience of *Brahman*. If Mother hits you, can you tell me how much pain you feel?

In the same way, one cannot possibly express *Brahman* through words.

Creation

Children, vibration arose in *Brahman* from Primordial Resolve. From this came the three gunas (qualities), *sattva*, *rajas* and *tamas*. These three are represented as the Trinity, Brahma, Vishnu and Shiva. All these are within oneself. What we see existing in the Universe in truth exists within.

On the relative plane, *Atman* is both *jivatma* (individual soul) and *Paramatma* (Supreme Soul). The individual soul is the enjoyer of the fruit of actions (karma). The Supreme Soul is the witness consciousness. It is actionless; it does not do anything.

Only when *Maya* ceases to delude us are we aware only of God. When we transcend *Maya* by constant spiritual practices, we will attain the state of *Brahman*. Not even a trace of *Maya* exists in *Brahman*.

Children, mitya does not mean non-existent, it means ever-changing. For example, first there is a grain of wheat, then wheat flour and finally bread. The substance does not become extinct.

However dirty the seashore may be, do we not enjoy the beauty of the sea? The mind does not get entangled in the litter. Like this, when the mind is fixed on God, it does not get ensnared by *Maya*.

We may consider a needle to be insignificant, saying it is cheap, yet the value of a thing is not determined by its cost but by its use. Mother does not see a needle as trivial. Whatever the object may be, we must consider its use not its cost. If we see things in this way, nothing is mitya.

Some people contend that creation has not taken place. In sleep we do not know anything. When we sleep there is no today, tomorrow, I, you, wife, son, body, etc. This is an example to show that *Brahman* still exists as *Brahman*. One may ask, "Is there not an entity that enjoys sleep and after waking says, 'I slept well'?" We say we slept well only because of the satisfaction and well-being that the body derives from sleep, not because "I" is present. The thought of "I-ness" and "my-ness" is the source of all our problems.

Rationalism

Children, because of quarrels created by religious dogmatics, is it rational to say that places of worship are not necessary? Would people argue that doctors and hospitals are not necessary because of the errors of a few doctors? Never. It is religious conflicts that need to be eliminated, not temples of God.

In former times rationalists loved the people, but what about today's rationalists? Posing as rationalists and inflating their egos, they trouble others. The real rationalist is one who holds onto his conviction dearly and loves others even at the cost of his own life. God kneels before that person. How many such people are there today?

When a theist (believer in God) develops devotion and reverence, qualities like love, truth, compassion, righteousness and justice will also develop in him. Anyone who approaches him feels solace and peace. This is the real benefit that the world derives from a believer in God. Today's rationalist does not study the scriptures properly but focuses on two or three words from some book and creates problems. This is why Mother says that the rationalism of today opens the way for a downfall.

Random Quotes

Children, Nature is a book to study; each object in nature is a page in that book.

Man's actions condition Nature's grace.

Sadhaks utilize the energy of Nature for meditation, for nourishment and for many other purposes. When we use ten percent of Nature's energy resources, we should devote at least one percent to the welfare of other people. Otherwise, what use is this life?

Children, nowadays there is a glut of

people giving spiritual discourses, yet no specific benefit from these talks can be seen. If the time spent preparing discourses were spent for meditation, people would receive some benefit. A person who has gained spiritual experience need not trouble his throat by giving discourses to inspire people. By his mere look thousands of people will turn to the right path. We cannot look at a clean mirror when the sun is reflected in it or our eyes will be blinded by the glare. In the same way, one cannot say anything against a real *sadhak* when face to face with him; one can only obey his word. Such is the power acquired through *sadhana*.

Children, we should not dislike those who do immoral acts. Our aversion should be toward their deeds, not towards them.

Water stagnates in ditches and ponds where germs and insects breed and afflict many people with diseases. The remedy is to channel the water to flow into the ocean. Today men live with so much ego; their impure thoughts cause many people to suffer. To broaden their narrow minds and to guide them to the Supreme Truth is our goal. For this, each one of us should be prepared to endure sacrifice. Only with the power acquired through *sadhana* should we lead them.

Children, eat to live; sleep to awaken.

We came from God. Faint awareness of this is present in us. This awareness should become full and complete.

There are many people around us who are struggling without a house, clothes, food and medical care. With the money you spend on smoking for one year, a small house could be built for a poor man. When we become compassionate toward the poor, our selfishness will disappear. We do not renounce anything but derive satisfaction from others' happiness. When we lose selfishness we become fit for God's Grace.

Children, only one who has studied can teach. Only one who has acquired can give. Only one who is completely free from sorrow can free others from sorrow completely.

Every place has a heart center where the full energy is gathered. India is the heart of the world. The *Sanatana Dharma* (Eternal Religion) which originated here is the source of all other paths. When the very word "*Bharatam*" (India) is heard, we feel the pulse of peace and effulgence. The reason is that India is the land of sages. They are the ones who transmit the life force not only to India, but to the whole world.

Gods & God

Question: *Mother, why is it necessary to worship God with form when He is really formless?*

Mother: Children, in order to get peace, we are in the habit of sharing our sorrows with our friends, whereas we should share our sorrows only with a Universal Being. This is the aim behind the worship of God with form.

Once Shiva and Parvati were sitting together when, suddenly, Shiva got up and ran off. But within a few minutes he was back at Parvati's side. "Why did You return so quickly?" She asked. "One of my devotees used to tell his sorrows only to me," Shiva began. "No matter what they were, he never shared them with anyone else. Today, when he was on his way home, some people mistook him for a thief and beat him up. Seeing this, I went to rescue him. But on my way there, I saw him talking to some other man. 'They beat me up for no reason,' he was saying, 'You should help me take revenge.' Since my help was not necessary, I returned."

Do not increase your sorrows by sharing them with others. Tell your problems to God; try to solve them in that way. If we share our sorrows with God alone, we will gain eternal peace.

An ordinary man may not develop love as easily for the formless aspect of God as he would if he worshipped God with form. Following the Path of Knowledge without devotion is like eating stones. The formless and omnipotent God can easily assume form for the sake of His devotees. If one has full faith and confidence in the form of his Beloved Deity, he can easily reach his goal. Still, we should worship God with the understanding that all deities are actually different aspects of the same God; and we should know that same God to be our own true Self.

Question: *If God is one and non-dual, why should we worship Shiva, Vishnu, and other such gods?*

Mother: The same actor plays many roles. Though his costumes and mannerisms may differ, the actor remains the same. God is like this. Truth is one; the names and forms are different. Men have different natures and characters. The different forms of God were set forth by the *Rishis* (ancient sages) to enable us to realize God by selecting those names and forms which appeal to our temperament. It is not that there are different gods. The sages have portrayed the non-dual God in different ways at different times according to the tastes and temperaments of people.

Question: *If God is one, then what is the*

need for separate places of worship for each religion?

Mother: Does an object change just because it is known by different names? Water may be called 'vellom' in Malayalam and 'pani' in Hindi, but does the colour and taste change? No. Is there any difference between the electric current which passes through the refrigerator, the lamp and the fan? No. Christians call God "Christ" and Muslims refer to God as "Allah". Each person understands and worships God according to his own cultural and religious traditions.

Question: *Mother, a lot of money is offered to God in temples in the name of puja and worship. What does God require money for?*

Mother: God does not need anything from us. An electric lamp does not require the help of a kerosene lantern. God is like the sun. He sheds light equally on all things in the world. Yet it is to this all-illuminating God that we offer a lamp and oil. This is done out of ignorance. It is like holding a burning candle up to the sun and saying, 'O Sun God, here is light for You to see Your path." The offerings we make in the temples are actually for our benefit. God is the giver of everything. He does not need or want anything from us.

Temples

Question: *What are temples for? Is not the sculptor who chiselled the beautiful idol the one who deserves to be adored?*

Mother: Just as we remember our father when we see his portrait, we are reminded of God, the Creator of the world, when we see the idol. When a devotee of Krishna sees the idol of Sri Krishna, he remembers the real Lord Krishna, not just the stone image. Temples and idols are needed for those of us who are steeped in ignorance.

Question: *Are temples necessary for re-membering God?*

Mother: When children are small, they study things by looking at pictures in books. These pictures help them to learn.

For instance, a child gets an idea of what a camel or a lizard is by seeing the picture of one. As he gets older, the child will grow to understand that the camel he sees in his book is only a picture. But when he is young, these pictures facilitate the development of his intellect. Similarly, temples can help us to remember God.

Question: *I have heard that if puja (daily worship,) is discontinued in temples, adverse reactions will occur. Is this true?*

Mother: As a result of man's resolve, the power of temple gods increases. If a *puja* is discontinued, that power diminishes. The power of the *devata* depends on the *bhavana* (resolve) of the person who installs it. Don't discontinue the daily worship performed in temples or that of the family deity. If these rites are dropped, great misfortune may befall us.

Suppose we feed a crow for ten days.

On the eleventh day if we don't feed it, it will follow us crowing. We will be unable to work attentively. If we stop the daily worship of devatas they will always trouble us in their subtle forms. This will affect weak-minded people a great deal, although a *sadhak* will not be affected much.

Building a boat is not enough; we should learn how to row. If we get into a boat without knowing how to row, it will float about randomly. Do we blame the boat if we have not learned how to row? Similarly, it is not enough to construct temples. We must look after them properly also. Daily worship should be performed; if not, misfortune may result. We are foolish to blame the temples then.

Question: *Are devatas (gods) and Isvara (God) different?*

Mother: Devatas are created and installed by man's *sankalpa* (resolve). Man's *sankalpa* has limitations, and his creations will reflect this. God, on the other hand, is all-powerful. His power neither increases nor decreases; it is eternal. The difference between the devatas and Isvara is like the difference between animals and man. Even though the essence of everything is the same, a dog does not have the discrimination of man. A dog loves only those who love him; he may bite others.

Question: *If devatas are different from God, won't temples become harmful to human beings?*

Mother: Temples where the devatas are worshipped properly will never become dangerous or harmful. But we should be a bit careful. Installations of devatas are often done by priests who are incapable of controlling their own *prana* (life force). The daily worship in such temples should never be stopped. Have you seen fish living in aquariums? The water must be changed daily; if it is not, it will be harmful to the fish. If the daily *puja* is performed properly, material prosperity will result.

The greatness of temples where Mahatmas have installed the idols is unique. They perform the installation with the *sankalpa* of Akhanda Satchitananda, giving divine power to the idols. These temples and their idols will be full of this divine power and light. They are not like aquariums and the fish that live there, but like fish that live in the river. In such temples, the daily *puja* will never be discontinued. Even if the *puja* were stopped, there would be no loss of power. These temples will be centers of great attraction and will have eternally auspicious attributes. Tirupathi, Guruvayur and Chottanikara temples are examples of this.

Question: *Why were human sacrifices conducted in temples?*

Mother: The ignorance of people in earlier times prompted them to perform such sacrifices. They believed that human sacrifices would please God. Misunderstanding the words of the scriptures, they performed these sacrifices. Look at our present day world. In the name of politics there is so much bloodshed. Atrocities like killing a man who changes political parties, killing the members of different political parties, shootings and stabbings are commonplace. Does any party's by-laws or ideology sanction murder or such atrocities? The manifesto and preachings of a party may be very good, but what they carry out is entirely different. In the same way, there were fools in those days whose blind devotion and belief prompted them to perform such acts.

Question: *Do these people incur sins?*

Mother: If they act for a universal cause, there is no sin, but if they act for a selfish end, they sin. Once there were two brahmins in a village. Both became afflicted with the same disease. When they consulted a doctor, he told them that if they ate fish they would be cured. As both were strict vegetarians, they were at their wits' end. The first man, yielding to the demand of his wife and children, ate fish and was cured. The second man, being afraid of sin, refused to take fish and died as a result. His family was deprived of his support and subjected to many troubles.

Here the first man who ate the comparatively insignificant fish protected his whole family. This is not cruelty. The second man refused to eat fish and died, leaving his whole family to suffer. A family is of far greater importance than one or two fish. Don't we cut down trees to build a house? This is not selfish. It is when we act with vengeance, motivated by likes and dislikes, that we sin.

Question: *Mother, what is the reason for the loss of sanctity in the temples?*

Mother: In the name of festivals, people collect money and conduct worldly programs in temples. This makes the surroundings of temples impure. Instead of cultivating devotion and good thoughts in people, such programs create vulgar thoughts and passions. What nonsense is done in the name of God! Collecting money for festivals, people get drunk and engage in fighting. In the temple precincts they conduct dramas, dance programs, and similar functions which arouse worldly thoughts in the minds of the audience. Young children are also be affected by this. At an age when good thoughts should be developing, these programs make them stray from the right path. These thought waves make the temple atmosphere unholy.

Children, we alone destroy ourselves. First we should become good. We should see that temples are kept pure. Only the arts of divine nature which increase devotion and faith should be permitted in temples. The daily *puja* should be done properly. If we make the temple surround-ings impure, there is no use accusing the devatas. In earlier times meditation, reading of the *Puranas*, *yogasanas*, etc., were practiced in temples. Only stories of God were presented as drama during festivals.

The money collected from the public for festivals can be utilized for humani-tarian purposes. There are so many people who are struggling without houses in our villages. We can build houses for them. We can give clothes and food in charity to the poor. We can help those who are unable to afford the costs of a marriage ceremony. Religious books can be printed and distributed free of charge and used for teaching children. Orphan-ages can be built. These children can be brought up with good culture and character. If we do this there will not be any orphans in the future. All these generous actions will help create unity among people.

Children, look at the Christians and Muslims and all the good things they do. They build orphanages and schools, teach orphans religion, and look after their needs. Have you seen any churches in a dilapidated condition? No. But see the plight of Hindu temples. So many temples remain uncared for and unattended. The Devaswom Board (government agency for maintenance of temples) takes over the management of big temples because they can make money, while they ignore small temples.

We should take special care to renovate temples and conduct divine arts during festival seasons. In cooperation with others we ourselves should take care of temples in the proper way. Their holiness should be preserved, otherwise our culture will degenerate.

Question: *Is it possible to attain Liberation through temple worship?*

Mother: It is possible, but one must worship with the understanding of the inner significance of the temples. God resides in temples, but don't think that He is limited by the four walls of a temple. Have firm belief that God is omnipresent. A bus will take us to the bus stop nearest our house; from there we can easily walk the remaining distance. Similarly, correct temple worship will take us to the threshold of *Satchitananda*; from there we have only a short distance to cover before we attain Perfection. You can take birth in a temple, but don't die there. That is to say that, in the beginning, a seeker can perform temple worship; it is a stepping stone, but the final and real goal is beyond all these things.

Mantra

Question: *Do words have the power to change the character of a person?*

Mother: Definitely. Once a brahmin was teaching spiritual matters to his students in a temple, when the king of the country arrived. The brahmin, engrossed in his teaching, was unaware of the king's arrival. The king became angry and berated the brahmin for not noticing him. The brahmin explained that as he was deeply involved with teaching, he was unaware of the king's arrival. The king then asked what the brahmin was teaching so earnestly that he was not aware of the king's presence. The brahmin replied, "I was teaching the children things which will purify their characters. These things must be taught with full attention and sincerity." The king mockingly asked, "Can mere words change the character?" The brahmin replied, "Certainly change will happen." The king retorted, "Character cannot change just like that." At that moment one of the brahmin's students, a small boy, ordered the king to get out of the temple. As soon as the king heard his words, he was enraged and roared, "How dare you say that! I will kill you, your Guru, and destroy this ashram as well!" Then the king caught hold of the brahmin who simply responded: "Please forgive me. You just now said that mere words cannot change the character of a person. Yet when a small boy said a few words to you you changed remarkably from your normal character. You were even ready to kill me and destroy everything."

Children, through words character can indeed be changed. If ordinary words can change one's character, then what of the power of a mantra which emanates from the *Rishis* and contains *bijaksharas* (seed letters, OM, HRIM, KLIM)?

Question: *Mother, does one benefit from chanting mantra?*

Mother: Definitely. But it is vital that a mantra be chanted with concentration. Depending on one's *bhavana* one will develop power. Mental attitude is the criterion. A doctor may prescribe medicine and tell the patient to rest and avoid certain foods. If the patient follows the instructions, his disease will be cured. Similarly, the *Rishis* have told us that if we chant a mantra in a prescribed way, certain results will naturally flow from the practice. If we follow their instructions meticulously, we will definitely obtain the fruit of chanting mantra.

Rituals

Question: *Mother, do the rituals performed during pitrukarma (ancestral ceremonies) have any effect?*

Mother: Children, pure *sankalpa* has great power, but only when *sankalpa* is pure do rituals bear fruit. When *pitrukarma* is performed, the name, birth, star, form and attitude of the dead person are remembered and the mantras chanted. Each ritual has its respective *devata*. Just as parents will receive a letter from their son in a distant place if it is properly addressed, the effect of rituals will also reach the intended person. If *sankalpa* is pure, the *devata* of that ritual will assure that its result will reach that particular soul.

Rishis (Sages)

Question: *What is the guarantee that the Rishis' predictions will come true?*

Mother: The ancient *Rishis* were mantra-drishtas (visionaries); whatever they said has come true. Everything written in the *Bhagavatam* about *Kaliyuga* has been accurate. "The father will eat the son; the son will eat the father. All the forests will become houses, all the houses will become shops." Are these things not happening? We cut down trees and build houses and shops in their place. Truth and dharma have no value at all. Is there mutual trust, love, sincerity, patience, sacrifice, in our world? Weather in both the rainy season and the sunny season is extreme. During the growing season, crops dry up for lack of rain. All these things were predicted by the sages.

The ancient *Rishis*, eating only leaves and fruits, did *tapas*, (severe austerities), and realized the Secret of the Universe. The whole Creation was like a mustard seed in the palm of their hand. Even inanimate objects obeyed their command. The *Rishis* made many discoveries in ancient times. Even present day inventions, which we consider to be very great, were brought forth effortlessly by them. For example, scientists have produced test tube babies. Yet the sage Vyasa brought forth one hundred and one Kauravas from clay pots; he imparted life to mere hunks of flesh. When compared with this, the test tube baby is nothing. In the *Ramayana*, reference is made to "*pushpaka vimana*",(airplane made of flowers), yet the modern airplane was invented only recently. There are many examples like these.

Mother does not consider present day scientists and their inventions to be insignificant, but rather these examples show that there is nothing that cannot be gained by *tapas*. For the *Rishis* all these things were quite simple; they were able to create anything through their *sankalpa*.

Devi Bhava

(Two nights a week, Mother outwardly manifests Her unity with the Supreme in Devi Bhava Darshana, (vision of the Divine Mother). Wearing brightly coloured saris and ornaments, she brings forth the form of Devi in full splendour and gives comfort and solace to the people.)

Question: *Why does Mother wear a costume during Devi Bhava? Sankaracharya, Ramakrishna Paramahamsa, Narayana Gurudev.... None of them wore such costumes.*

Mother: If all Gurus/Saints were alike, then Sankaracharya would have been enough; he alone could have uplifted the world. One person is not like another. Saints and *Avatars* will also differ. Sri Rama was not like Sri Krishna; Ramana Maharshi was not like Ramakrishna Paramahamsa. Each Incarnation takes birth for a different reason; each has a different purpose to fulfill, and will make use of different methods to do so. If all of them had identical roles, one Mahatma alone would have sufficed to uplift the world. One man need not be like another.

Children, when we see a lawyer's garb we are reminded of our case and its success. When we see the postman we are reminded of letters. Mother's dress is to remind you of the Supreme. Here is a story.

Once a leader was invited to a conference. He arrived in the clothing of an ordinary man. The people who arranged the meeting refused to receive him or allow him to enter. The leader went home and dressed himself in pants, coat, shoes, etc. When he returned to the meeting he was welcomed and served a sumptuous meal. The leader removed his clothing and placed the items in front of the food. Amazed at such an act, the hosts asked the reason. The leader replied, "When I came in the clothing of an ordinary man, you did not respect me. When I came well-dressed, you welcomed me. What you respect and welcome is the clothing and not me, so let this clothing eat the food."

The world respects only the costume; this is the reason Mother wears Her present dress. The visual appearance of Mother in Devi Bhava is to release us from our limited perception of our Self and remind us of the Supreme which is our True Nature.

Love

Children, don't waste the time you have been given by God. Take refuge in the Universal Mother. Only Mother loves us selflessly. To think that many people love us is a wrong notion; their love is selfish. Mother will tell you a story to explain this.

Once, a father and his daughter set out on a journey. They travelled all day long and saw many beautiful places along the way. In the evening they reached a hotel where they could rest for the night. The moment the hotel owner saw them, he welcomed them with great love and respect. Two or three attendants appeared to serve them and immediately took them to a well-furnished room and brought them food. The attendants cheerfully took their dirty clothes and returned them nicely washed and ironed, offering them hot water for their bath and doing whatever the guests wished. That night, musicians sang and played musical instruments for them.

The next morning, as the father and daughter prepared to leave, the daughter exclaimed, "Father, how kind these people are!" Before he could answer her, a servant arrived to present the hotel bill. The father told his daughter, "This bill is for the love and service they rendered us. They charged us for every service rendered. Their love is based on selfishness."

Children, love is like this. The mutual love that people seem to show arises from selfishness. When a person goes against our wishes, we withdraw our love. Selfless love flows only from God, the Embodiment of Love. Know this and realize God. Properly utilize the Essence within.

Anger

Question: *No matter how much I meditate and do japa, I don't seem to be gaining any benefit. Why is this so?*

Mother: Children, we go to a temple with devotion for worship. Having devotedly circumambulated the temple, we stand before the Deity to worship. Suppose somebody comes and stands in front of us and obstructs our view? Immediately we get angry. Then all the energy gained by our concentration up to that time is dissipated. Even if God Himself comes disguised, we would get angry with Him. This is our habit. Then how can we gain any benefit by doing *japa* and meditation? The benefit gained through good thoughts is lost in many ways, through anger, lust, greed, jealousy, and so forth. We should remember this. A spiritual aspirant should never get angry. When we get angry, much of the energy and power gained by *sadhana* is drained away. Only with great *sraddha* can a spiritual aspirant reach the goal. Whatever we see or hear, we should think it over in solitude. Only then should we make a decision. Never become a slave to circumstances; try to overcome them.

"I Am Brahman"

Question: *Mother, I am Brahman, so why should I perform sadhana?*

Mother: Children, without being called by your name, can you respond? Now we are at the level of name. Don't you have yesterday, today, tomorrow, you, me, 'my' house, wife, children, taste, distaste? The present state of your *Brahman* is like an animal without discrimination. It is also *Brahman*. That is your present state. Don't live saying, "I am *Brahman*", simply reading the words of the *Rishis* which were written from their direct experience. To say "I am *Brahman*" after reading some books is like a watchman who takes pride in saying that the property which he guards is his own. Jackfruit may say, "I am *Brahman*" yet its seed will stay the same. You are only the seed. Through *sadhana* you can realize *Brahman*.

Children, *Brahman* is to be experienced and cannot be expressed through words. Once a rishi sent his son to a *gurukula* for studies. After completing twelve years of study, the son returned and proudly told his father, "Do you know who I am? I am the embodiment of *Brahman*," and started behaving with ego. Seeing his child acting egotistically, the rishi felt pity for him. He asked his son to bring some milk and sugar candy and told him to dissolve the rock sugar in the milk. When this was done, the rishi took some milk from the middle portion and, pouring it into his son's mouth, asked whether it was sweet. His son answered 'yes'. Taking milk from the top this time, the rishi poured it into his mouth and asked whether it was sweet. The son again answered yes. Then the rishi gave him the following advice:

"Son, *Brahman* cannot be expressed in words. Though *Brahman* pervades everything, It must be known in the realm of experience. "Without realizing *Brahman*, do not go on saying, "I am *Brahman*."

Children, a learned man was walking through the streets singing, "Everything is *Brahman*". A man who saw this took a thorn and pricked the pundit from behind. The pundit cried out from pain and angrily shouted, "Who is that?" He chased the man to beat him up. Children, our *Brahman* is like this, the moaning *Brahman*.

Now listen to the tale of a Self-Realized man. A Mahatma was walking down the street singing, "Everything is *Brahman*." A man came from behind and cut his arm. The Mahatma, unaware of his injury, continued walking and singing, oblivious of everything. The man who attacked him then understood that he was a Mahatma. Feeling deep remorse, he approached the Mahatma and begged his forgiveness. The Mahatma asked, "What for?" The man replied, "For cutting your arm." Only then the Mahatma discovered his injury. Rubbing the wound, he restored his arm to its normal state. Then the Mahatma said, "Even though I was singing 'Everything is Brahman', I had to do the action of rubbing to make the arm well. Still I remain on the level of action."

Children, we have no right to say 'I am Brahman' except through experience. Without trying to become the pundit, try to become the Mahatma who realized Truth through experience.

Glossary

Advaita: *Philosophy of Non-duality*

Akhanda Satchitananda: *Undivided Being-Awareness-Bliss*

Asana: *Sitting posture for meditation*

Atman: *The Self*

Avatar: *Incarnation of God*

Bharatam: *India*

Bhava Roga: *Disease of 'becoming' (transmigration)*

Bhajan: *Devotional singing*

Bhakti: *Devotion*

Bhakti Yoga: *The Path of Yoga through devotion*

Bhavana: *Mood, attitude*

Bhavaroga: *The disease of becoming*

Bhaya Bhakti: *Devotion with fear, awe and reverence*

Bijaksharas: *Seed letters of mantras, e.g. hrim, klim, aim, om*

Brahma: *God of Creation*

Brahman: *The Absolute*

Brahmacharya: *Training in discipline and self-restraint, celibacy*

Darshan: *Vision or audience of a saint or God*
Devata: *Minor god or goddess*
Devi: *Divine Mother, Goddess*
Dhyana: *Meditation*
Diksha: *Initiation*
Ekadasi: *Eleventh day of the lunar month*
Guna: *Quality, attribute (see tamas, rajas)*
Guru: *Spiritual Master, preceptor*
Gurukula: *Institution of learning run by a Guru*
Homa: *Vedic sacrifice using the medium of fire*
Ishta Devata: *Beloved or Chosen Deity*
Isvara: *God, Lord*
Janma: *A birth or lifetime*
Japa: *Repetition of a mantra or Divine Name*
Jiva: *Individual soul*
Jivanmukta: *Liberated soul*
Jivanmukti: *Liberation of the soul while living in the body*
Jivatma: *Individual self*
Jñana: *Knowledge (of the Self)*
Jñna Yoga: *The Yoga of Knowledge*
Kaliyuga: *Dark Age of materialism*
Karma: *Action*
Karma Yoga: *Yoga through detached actions*
Kumbaka: *Retention of breath during pranayama*

Lakshya Bodha: *Awareness of or inclination towards the Goal of God-Realization*

Mahatma: *Literally, Great Soul, also a Realized Being*

Mala: *Rosary, strand of 108 beads used for japa*

Mantra: *Sacred or mystic formula or combination of words which, if repeated, bestows spiritual power and purity*

Mantra Drishtas: *Sages who visualized mantras*

Maya: *Universal Illusion*

Mitya: *Ever-changing, non-eternal*

Nirvikalpa Samadhi: *State of oneness with the Absolute*

Nitya: *Eternal*

Ojas: *Sublimated vital force*

Paramatma: Supreme Self

Pitru Karma: *Religious ceremonies for the departed*

Prana: *Vital force*

Pranayama: *Breathing exercises for gaining control over the prana*

Puja: *Worship*

Puranas: *Ancient epics*

Pushpaka vimana: *A famous airplane figuring in the Ramayana*

Rajas: *The 'guna' of activity*
Ramayana: *Epic story of Sri Rama*
Rishi: *Ancient seer*
Satguru: *Realized Master*
Sadhak: *Spiritual aspirant*
Sadhana: *Spiritual practices*
Sahaja Samadhi: *Natural abidance in the Self*
Sahasranamam: *The 1000 Names of God*
Samadhi: *Union with Reality*
Samsara: *Cycle of birth, death, and rebirth*
Samskara: *Latent tendency of the mind*
Sanatana Dharma: *The Eternal Religion of the Vedas*
Sankalpa: *A resolve*
Sannyasi: *A renunciate*
Satchitananda:
Pure Being-Awareness-Bliss
Satsang: *Keeping holy company*
Sattvic: *'Guna' of purity or clarity*
Savasana: *Yogic posture of corpse pose*
Savikalpa Samadhi: *Perception of Reality while retaining the sense of duality*
Shakti: *Essential Power of the Universe associated with the feminine aspect of the Absolute*
Siddha: *Oushada: Perfect medicine*
Siddhis: *Psychic powers*
Sraddha: *Faith or attention, care*

Srimad Bhagavatam: *Holy scripture of Lord Sri Krishna's life, deeds and teachings*

Tamas: *'Guna' of dullness*

Tapas: *Austerities, penance*

Upadesa: *Advice or teaching*

Vasanas: *Innate tendencies of the mind accumulated during this and previous births, e.g., anger, lust, greed, jealousy, etc.*

Vishnu: *God of Preservation*

Yaga: *Vedic sacrifice*

Yogasanas: *Yogic postures*